Ach, any fool can write a book

Etienne MARADENE

**ACH, ANY FOOL CAN
WRITE A BOOK**

ETIENNE MARADENE

Martin Martin wanted to visit St Kilda. St Kilda is the western island the most westerly of Scotland's, the farthest away from the Hebrides. Authors having published something about St Kilda before him had not visited it. So when in 1696 the opportunity arose to go there, he did not hesitate one moment and at once went aboard. From his journey he wrote a book in the anthropological and scientific manner of his time for the Royal Society.

Samuel Johnson was born in 1709, of a second hand bookseller father who put Martin Martin's book into his hands. The young Samuel devoured it.

James Boswell was a well-educated Scot aristocrat, who also had read Martin Martin. When in 1763 he met Samuel Johnson in London, Johnson had become a "Sir", an acknowledged lexicographer with a royal pension, literary critic, "the" reviewer of his time, conversationalist, witty and feared social animal; he fell in love with him, of the love of the disciple towards his revered master. Ten years later the disciple managed to make his ageing master, 64 years old, to temporarily abandon the London he loved, for a journey to Scotland and the Hebrides. So together during eighty four days, from Wednesday August 18th to Tuesday November 9th 1773, they visited Scotland and the Scots in Scotland and the Hebrides. From their tour both of them wrote a journal. Johnson's, published in 1775, is not a literary masterpiece, but rather an interesting document for the study of eighteenth century English prejudices! Boswell's, published one year after the death of his beloved Johnson, which occurred in 1784, is a gem of the Anglo-Saxon literature!

Colin Mackenzie was my father-in-law. In 1991 he put into my hands Boswell's journal entitled "The Journal of a Tour to the Hebrides with Samuel Johnson", it was love at first sight! When later I became a late student, and was asked to propose a topic for a memoir, instantly I thought of Boswell, of his trip with Johnson.

In 2011 we bought a mobile home van, and in summer hup, my wife Françoise and I followed Boswell and Johnson's footsteps. In 1773 they respectively were 33 and 64 years old, in 2011 Françoise and Etienne were respectively 58 and 60 years old.

WALKING UP THE HIGH STREET.

Tantallon, Cockenzie, Edinburgh, Linlithgow

Scotland's capital city. Let's read again their journals. Johnson's does not say a word about it! But Boswell instead takes this opportunity to tell us about the incentive for their trip: *Dr. JOHNSON had for many years given me hopes that we should go together, and visit the Hebrides. Martin's Account of those islands had impressed us with a notion that we might there contemplate a system of life almost totally different from what we had been accustomed to see; and, to find simplicity and wildness, and all the circumstances of remote time or place, so near to our native great island, was an object within the reach of reasonable curiosity.*

From which we understand that even for Boswell who is Scot, there is a chasm between them, well educated people, and the Scotland they propose to visit, analyse and understand in the investigating scientific style of the Enlightenment, the Scotland described by Martin Martin 77 years earlier. However this Scotland is not any more Martin Martin's one, because during these 77 years it underwent two superimposed traumatic changes with durable consequences: the Act of Union and the Culloden defeat. The Act of Union dates back from 1707, and without entering into details, one can say that it confirmed the de facto scission existing between Lowlands and Highlands. So we understand that Boswell is curious of this other Scotland, Highlanders' one, because he himself is a Lowlander, and that there is a misunderstanding between these two worlds. To make simple let's say that Lowlanders treat with the English, are somehow in an acculturating process, have adopted the English points of view, principles, way of life. Of course, only aristocrats are concerned, but they set the tune. Conversely Highlanders remain independent and proud to be so, in love with and attached to their culture. On the one hand you have the minions, on the other hand the unyielding sovereignists. Politically speaking, the Act of Union puts Scotland and England under a same and single government's authority, which is not something benign! As for Culloden, it is even worse. There, at Culloden, the Highlanders' last hopes of independence, and those who dared to follow Charles Edward Stuart in his rash adventure to grasp both England and Scotland's crowns, were irretrievably crushed in 1746. And it is only twenty seven years later that Boswell and Johnson tour the highlands. The wound is still open and cankering, all the more cankering that the English determination to eradicate all possible future uprisings is fierce. Their present Scotland is a savagely mutilated and persecuted land, and when following their steps, the watermark of this tragedy will become obvious. Let us now shut this parenthesis and come back to what Boswell tells us. In a nutshell he says that from having read Martin Martin, they think that not too far from home, they have a good opportunity to travel back in time and survey a way of life totally different from theirs.

And as for us, what did we do, what did we see in Edinburgh? We were there the 23rd of July 2011, fair weather, and after having somehow lost our way round the harbour on the mouth of the river Leith, which is nice indeed because I wanted to have an idea of the place from which they had left Edinburgh and boarded a ship to start out on the 18th of August 1773, we politely asked the Miss who patiently inhabits the small box I regularly stick to the bottom of the windscreen with the help of a sucker, how to go to the castle, and politely too she guided us, street by street, crossing by crossing, roundabout by roundabout, left right straight ahead, bear right bear left, stoical, make a U-turn when possible, never cross, recalculating, and scientifically, methodically, in constant communication with orbiting artificial satellites geographically still at somehow 36.000 kilometres above Edinburgh, she took us to the castle where for few days Bonnie Prince Charlie was King!

Inside this castle, nothing about Boswell, nothing about Johnson, but war war war, glorious wars, glorious soldiers, glorious stupidity of institutionalised violence, and at the very top a Christian church whose love message is generously genuinely warped beyond recognition into a war cry, a war message, a war auto-satisfaction, a war divine mission, a war culture. There, under fake contrition, WAR is obviously adored! Ach, we feel sick! But there are a lot of tourists, and Chinese tourists, and this is new, and to me who is learning Chinese, funny. As usual they are like Italians, very talkative and even noisy, "look at this, look at that", "tell father, tell mother", "oh oh, toilets are here!" etc., and they love to take photos of themselves in front of the Anglo-Scot temple of occidental violence, of war. How far it is from the opium wars, when this same violence, sneaking its way up their rivers with gunboats, made them bow to unfair treaties, to the gunboat policy.

Christian gunboat policy? Yes, says Edinburgh castle! Then on our way back we take photos of a restaurant plaque boasting of the fact that Boswell and Johnson "are reputed to have met and dined in this building circa 1770". I find this "circa" dubious, as we know perfectly well that they were in Edinburgh in 1773! Never mind. We also visit The Writers' Museum, where on display are Robert Burns, Sir Walter Scott, Robert Louis Stevenson, but no James Boswell! It is here that as a decorative frieze under the toilets' ceiling I find the title of my book "Ach, any fool can write a book". Then with a take-away fish and chips, back to our vehicle. We bought it from a Tandoori and Kebab shop, which is the norm today. Our world is slightly changing, which is nice indeed.

Late afternoon the day before, we had visited Tantallon castle, where the man at the desk, historian selling tickets, had suggested a pass ticket for several historical sites, which we had bought. And a good idea it was, because thanks to this ticket we did not have to queue the long queue there was to visit the uninteresting Edinburgh castle. But there in Tantallon, we had a very good introduction to medieval Scotland, and the spell had been to observe swallows nesting here, so further from Africa than ours, elegantly jumping over the tall stern walls to reach the mild and warm sunny side, where insects harvesting was easier. But what a flaw in nature, what a breach of harmony, that life must be sustained at the expense of deaths! Then we had driven to Cockenzie and Port Seton, and parked in front of the Firth of Forth. Meal taken in the comfort of our wheeled little house, with a gorgeous radiant sunset over the firth, two rowing boats evening exercising, then a short walk on the narrow strip of beach, dipping fingers inside the North Sea, then after having observed a group of teenagers playing a teenagers' game of relentlessly throwing a ball into the waves, that one of them relentlessly strove to retrieve at the risk of being drenched, which happened of course, two of his friends then joyfully ineffectually wrenching water out of his tee-shirt, we drew our feathered nest's shutters and limply fell into Morpheus' arms, who here also between buildings was potent.

So, after the visit of Edinburgh castle, strong of our pass ticket we also visited Linlithgow palace where most of the Stuart had lived. The last of the Stuart to visit it is Bonnie Prince Charlie of course. And the 1st of February 1746, leaving the palace to wend to Culloden, the naughty Englishman the Duke of Cumberland set it on fire! Always the same story… So, what we can see of it today is about what was left of it then, enough of it to allow imagination to run rife; and snuggle myself inside the recess of the King's bedroom's hearth, where he used to sit to warm himself, with a fire-extinguisher servant standing in front of him with a ready bucket of water, has been to me the opportunity of an arch enjoyment!

…not have to queue…

…I find this "circa" dubious…

Inchkeith

Then we crossed the firth of Forth. "Firth" is the Scottish equivalent for fjord, and "Forth" is the name of the river flowing into this firth. Until 1890 it could be crossed only by boat, then thanks to a beautiful metalwork bridge still being in use today, it was possible to cross it by train. It is only in 1964 that the road spanned it with a suspension bridge, the one over which we drove. Our associates, of course, had crossed it by boat. They had taken this opportunity to land at and visit the small island of Inchkeith. Johnson gives a negative account of it, to him nothing is right on this little island, a mere rock with so thin a soil, nothing grows but thistles, and he reproaches to his companions their past lack of curiosity for this horrible place. It is interesting to compare their accounts, and appraise how the choice of words weighs this way or the other in the rendering of a place.

Johnson:

As we crossed the *Frith* of *Forth*, our curiosity was attracted by *Inch Keith*, a small island, which neither of my companions had ever visited, though, lying within their view, it had all their lives solicited their notice. Here, by climbing with some difficulty over shattered crags, we made the first experiment of unfrequented coasts. Inch Keith is nothing more than a rock covered with a thin layer of earth, not wholly bare of grass, and very fertile of thistles. A small herd of cows grazes annually upon it in the summer. It seems never to have afforded to man or beast a permanent habitation. We found only the ruins of a small fort, not so injured by time but that it might be easily restored to its former state. It seems never to have been intended as a place of strength, nor was built to endure a siege, but merely to afford cover to a few soldiers, who perhaps had the charge of a battery, or were stationed to give signals of approaching danger. There is therefore no provision of water within the walls, though the spring is so near, that it might have been easily enclosed. One of the stones had this inscription: 'Maria Reg.1564.' It has probably been neglected from the time that the whole island had the same king.

And Boswell:

In crossing the Frith, Dr. Johnson determined that we should land upon Inch Keith. On approaching it, we first observed a high rocky shore. We coasted about, and put into a little bay on the North-west. We clambered up a very steep ascent, on which was very good grass, but rather a profusion of thistles. There were sixteen head of black cattle grazing upon the island. Lord Hailes observed to me, that Brantome calls it *L'isle des Chevaux*, and that it was probably '*a safer* stable' than many others in his time. The fort, with an inscription on it, *Maria Re* 1564, is strongly built. Dr. Johnson examined it with much attention. He stalked like a giant among the luxuriant thistles and nettles. There are three wells in the island; but we could not find one in the fort. There must probably have been one, though now filled up, as a garrison could not subsist without it.

Isn't it cogent? Johnson is obviously in a moralistic negative vein!

Kinghorn, Kirkcaldy, Cupar

As for us, only us, once having crossed the Firth of Forth over the big bridge, we struggled to leave the main road, the too big too large too fast main road, monotonous main road, leisure-less road, landscape-less road, for by-roads. We somehow lost our way under both bridges, road and rail's, then thanks to perseverance, managed to strike a road allowing us to follow the coast eastwards towards Kinghorn. There we found a small car park overlooking the bay and Inchkeith, which in fact was not far from the shore. A wonderful view over sea, island, harbour.

For the first time I put on the Highlander dress we had bought from an Edinburgh tourist shop, of course it is a Mackenzie's, as my wife is a genuine Mackenzie! You are not without knowing that each clan has a tartan, with its own particular pattern and colours, worn only by members of the clan. Along with it there are a motto and a war cry, ours is *Tulach Ard*, 'High hill', and our motto *Luceo non uro*, 'I shine not burn', that my father in law Colin Mackenzie used to maliciously warp into 'I burn not shine'! Be informed that my way of wearing the kilt is warrior like, that is to say without underwear. In full dress I pose, and Françoise Mackenzie takes a photo of her "Highlander".

From Johnson's journal we know that they found post-chaise in Kinghorn. From Boswell's that they also dined there. They went through Kinghorn, Kirkaldy and Cowpar, which on our map are Kinghorn, Kirkcaldy and Cupar. They stopped at Cupar and drank tea, then rode by night to St Andrews where they arrived late. Concerning this Cupar, something funny happened to us, which I think is worth relating. When driving from Kinghorn to St Andrews, I was ignorant of their Cupar teatime, and while still at Kirkcaldy I programmed our Global Positioning System, (Satnav), to go to St Andrews. As all Satnav users know, when you do not have a precise address to feed your Satnav with, you usually pick up a common one like something-Square, or something-Church, what I certainly did. Then I dutifully followed the Satnav's injunctions, and after a while realised not driving on the 915 as intended, but on the 916 instead, these being road numbers! By the way, 916 is a charming narrow road. Being a narrow road in Scotland is an easy and common state, what is far less common and easy is to be wide enough to match French standard! And this very road 916, though narrow, led us through a charming countryside to Cupar where they had drunk tea. Indeed the address I had used was on the 91, between Cupar and St Andrews, a detour it seems, via this 916, difficult but charming.

But no, this is only appearance in a world of appearances! It is only when at St Andrews, re-reading their journals that I discovered that they had driven through Cupar and drunk tea there. Consequently,

reality versus appearances, is that at Kirkcaldy a ghost had taken us over, guided our
mistake, so that we could follow their steps,
and avoid missing Cupar where they had
had tea. It is a well-known fact that Scotland is rife with ghosts, and this very one,
as we shall see, stuck to us. But where had
we met her, him? Was it at Tantallon or at
Linlithgow, surely in one of these castles!

Tantallon castle

St Andrews

Is mind a product of brain? Probably yes, but difficult to admit it, the same with the concept of ghost, and however quite by chance we stop right in front of the university! It is the oldest one in Scotland, 1413, born in troubled times, when Christianity was cleft in two papacies, one pope being exiled in Spain (Benedict XIII), and Scotland had remained faithful to him, as well as King James, who was in an English jail. Since three years though, a bunch of Paris graduated teachers—at that time students had to study abroad—had set up a school, but they still needed a pope's authorisation to obtain the status of university. This exiled pope was willing to reward Scotland for her faithfulness, and granted it. Whew!

Teach, transmit, at that time art and religion—to each time its priorities—

spearhead of our species brimming with its voluminous brain. Of course a man of culture and learning like Johnson was receptive to it, all the more so as they were hosted by a university teacher, Dr. Watson.

In St Andrews, the cathedral's ruins are quite impressive. Ruined cathedrals are far more beautiful than standing ones. This is no irony! Soaring remaining pillars, incomplete ogives, gaping rosettes, ripped open gates, everything everywhere is an invitation towards the sky, towards up open sky, inviting welcoming wide open heavens. The architect of time has surpassed the human architect, respecting its spirit though, embellishing it, and caricaturing it. From the midst of these ruins, chants and prayers soar towards an unimpeded sky, limitless, like the religious preoccupations of Boswell and Johnson's ancestors were! At St Andrews, to sculpt the cathedral into its present state, the architect of time has had the unqualified help of a certain John Knox, hero of the Reformation, Calvin's comparable contemporary. Incensed by

Knox's sermons, a crowd of fanatics target-
ed one of the best cathedrals of pre-
Reformation Scotland, and instead of kneel-
ing and praying like legions of pilgrims had
done there before them, the 14th of June
1559, they rushed and destroyed it! And
this is how during a few years span, cathedrals destroyers destroyed them all but one,
Glasgow's, thanks to a clever guy, clever
and keen in communication, who told them:
*But no! This is not a Cathedral, just three
churches that have been stitched together!*
Voilà! But at St Andrews today, tourists
can enjoy these ruins, wonderfully set off
by impeccable Scot lawns, of such a vivid
green and soft thread as to make French
southerners dream!

There is also a castle on the edge of
water, where thirteen years earlier in 1546,
Cardinal David Beaton, bishop of Mirepoix
France, archbishop of St Andrews, was
murdered by Protestants. Three months
earlier he himself had ordered to burn a re-
formist preacher, George Wishart! Violence loves violence. And Knox who had

been a disciple of Wishart came to help occupy the site, retaken one year later by the earl of Arran assisted by a French naval force. You can visit the castle, also embellished by a magnificent lawn, in place and lieu of the brambles Johnson complained about, and crawl through mine and countermine rediscovered in 1879, impressive example of medieval sappers' work.

Boswell and Johnson slept two nights at St Andrews, August 18th and 19th. Johnson left St Andrews with a feeling of general decline, religious, academic, commercial, and even environmental, without trees! We leave it with a feeling of a healthy town.

Leuchars, Dundee, Carnoustie, Arbroath

They left St Andrews around noon, and not too far away they noticed a church with an old tower, they stopped to have a look at it. It was at Leuchars. There they asked the minister about this tower, he was a *very civil old man*, but did not know much about it. We also entered the church, and found there a plaque with the succession of ministers, and discovered the name of the *very civil old man* they had not named, Mister James Walker, minister there from 1733 to 1774, when Thomas Kettle succeeded him. Wonderful!

They ferried across the Firth of Tay, we 'bridged' it. At Dundee nothing special for them, nor for us. They went as far as Arbroath, as for us we stopped in a campsite at Carnoustie. It is a fact that in Scotland today Country music is loved, in toilets and showers the radio broadcasted a lot. But after seven nights 'wild', a comfortable campsite is deemed luxury, whatever the music…

The morrow we visited Arbroath Abbey. These ruins are really impressive, presented in a far more favourable light than in their time, many people having worked to understand and explain them. Johnson had guessed that it would be so: *Men skilled in architecture might do what we did not attempt: They might probably form an exact ground-plot of this venerable edifice. They may from some parts yet standing conjecture its general form, and perhaps by comparing it with other buildings of the same kind and the same age, attain an idea very near to truth.* And it is only in an underground dark remote corner of one of the buildings, that I find a small board laconically indicating Boswell and Johnson's visit in 1773. The adjoining museum is interesting, but how much wars, battles, violence…

Leuchars

1695 George Gordon
1706 James Robertson
1733 James Walker
1774 Thomas Kettle
1809 David Watson
1866 Robert Johnson

Montrose, Aberdeen, Cruden Bay

At Montrose they visited the English chapel. Johnson was a staunch Anglican. In reality whatever he thought or believed, it was staunchly! He was not so much of a doubter. Boswell on the contrary was an inveterate one, was God a reality? Were his contemporary philosophers believers or not? He had visited Rousseau, had become friend with him, had told him about his trifling with Catholicism, his idea of entering a monastery, and finally had yielded to his haunting thought and asked "Are you a Christian?" Rousseau had answered "Yes", even if anticlerical he thought himself a Christian! Then he had fallen in love with the giant Johnson, because *he* did not doubt, because enlightened Johnson considered religion one notch above reason. It was somehow contradictory in Johnson, but to what extreme would not one concede to cure one's anguishes?

Consort with staunch Johnson was Boswell's medicine…

As for us at Montrose we picnicked next to Bamse's statue, a star dog, World War II, Norwegian crew. Bamse had been a city VIP, had free bus transportation, everybody knew him, and his high feats in the rescuing business of humans had won him near citizenship!

From Montrose we followed the coastal road until Aberdeen, rainy and not hot. We did not go to Laurence-kirk where they had visited Lord Monboddo. It is a mistake, small one, but a mistake however. Perhaps that our guiding-ghost had a grudge against this place? Or we did not hear it because of the rain patter? Who knows? We will have to go back there!

At Aberdeen we stopped, food-shopped, and toured the "charities". Charity-shops are an Anglo-Saxon's peculiarity. I do not know a French equivalent for them. These are shops, most of the time small, often untidy, somehow old and dark, with at the till an old woman, who even if an elderly with arthritis and hunched and short-sighted with thick spectacles, is always neatly dressed and brimming with wit and humour. On sale are only second-hand articles, clothes, shoes, outmoded bibelots, books, VCRs and sometimes DVDs. Each charity has its raison d'être, cancer, Aids, heart, etc., and items are cheap and hand-written labelled. It is charming, soft, kind-hearted, nostalgic, principally voluntary, and this is the concept, no commercial competition, no venal aggressiveness, no mercantilism, only friendship, fatalism and recycling. And each time we unearth treasures, my wife amongst bibelots, always as intended gifts, and myself amongst books, always factual. Then when we collate our purchases, we are used to call them "spoils". At Aberdeen our spoils were great!

We had also bought some unsophisticated Scotch pastries, sweet, soft, sticky to fingers, and as when leaving Aberdeen

there was a traffic jam before the bridge
over the river Don, and that it was about
teatime, we sneaked off inside a narrow
lane on the left, squeezed up between
parked cars and a tall wall, reached the top
and turned right where we could park
alongside the pavement, swing our swing-
ing seats, boil some water, and sheltered
from the cold drizzle, leisurely drink in the
cosy inside of our travelling bubble, a hot
tea with Scotch pastries upon which we
abundantly commented.

Once the emptying office rush hour
had passed, we resumed our northern route
by following the shore until Cruden Bay,
where on the quay of the tiny Errol harbour,
between tides subjected dock and naturally
flowing river, we settled for the night. But
first, while Françoise is preparing a good
hot supper indoors, I, affronting drizzle
wind and cold, go scout the place. On one
side, like giant cobwebs hanging from
posts, are fishing nets, and facing the bay, a
row of houses along the stream. On the
other side there is a small dock, a neat

square of grey water dotted by a colourful flotilla. And clambering the north hill which protects dock, village, stream and bay, I discern seemingly nearby a castle, Slains castle.

Slain castle, Dun Bay, Bullers of Buchan

Night is falling now, cosy inside our camper our meal is drawing to a close, suddenly a car comes and parks just beside us, and another one, and another one, tackle is pulled out of the boots, and fishermen set up while chatting! Unexpected, but interesting. Then I step out with a box of Calissons d'Aix, and offer the sweets around. The almond paste elicits some commentaries from them, and dialogue is established. So I learn that the net at the dock's entrance is for salmons, that the electrical box on the quay is a killer whale cry emitter to keep seals away, particularly this bobbing head they point to me and that I can now see up and down the surface indeed, that salmons do not take food while migrating, consequently they could not fish them tonight with their lines, but that eels do eat, as well as plenty of other good fish they catch for their pleasure, fill deep freezers at home with, give to their families, and friends, and workmates. All of them work for Shell or Esso or what not, offshore or not, but deep in the petrol industry, and when I ask whether with theses riches buried under their feet they do not think of independence, one of them, as if in the know and with a secretive twist answers: "We are working on it!"[1].

I tell them about my quest of Slains castle, and also the Bullers of Buchan and Dun Buy, the yellow rock in Gaelic, thus baptised because numerous inhabiting birds stain it yellow with their guano. All of them know Slains castle and the Bullers or Buchan, also called Bouilloir of Buchan, but not Dun Buy, except for one of them who gives us directions on how to go there. Easy, but you have to know it! From the small car-park along the road, instead of

---

[1] But they just had their say, the 18th of September 2014, and disappointingly answered "NO"! What a pity!

walking right towards the castle, you need to go straight to the sea, then turn left northward, then from afar you can hear a distinctive rumble from the multitude of seabirds living there, upon a rock severed from the shoreline. The rumble amounts to a roar when near, and their ceaseless ballet is quite impressive, something up to now I had only seen through televised documentaries. Then through the wet grass I retrace my steps, walk along the shore to the castle where the countess Errol had hosted them so well, and had forbidden them to leave without having seen the Bouilloir of Buchan and Dun Buy. The Bouilloir of Buchan is like a gaping crater at the top of a cliff, with at its bottom an entrance-exit between sea and a waves agitated interior lake, of which airspace is constantly slowly majestically crossed by ever present seabirds. My shoes were drenched, the narrow footpath circling the crater as well, buried in ferns, with falling slopes towards the agitated lake on one side and the boiling sea on the other, I did not dare to follow it as they bravely did in 1773!

The castle is imposing. I approach it from the north, an elongated silhouette profuse in buildings. Wind is whistling past my face. It seemed near but was not. When reaching it I discover that it is built on a rocky spur, a splinter lodged into the flesh of a bristling Scottish shore, protruding at sea. I have no other option that skirt circumvent the invading sea-arm, and gain entrance through the southern part of the castle, its precipitous tower extending above the sea cliff. From these windows, contemplate the sea, appraise its mood, admire and fear its furies, must have been a long hours toll exacted from the life of the resident folk, comprising servants sustaining their hierarchically superior employers.

Oh this castle is derelict... surrounded by high wire nettings... to enter it is expressly forbidden... but there along the proud tower... the wire netting is ripped... an invisible outstretched hand invites me to squeeze through, to come in without permission, I am already upstairs the spiral staircase! Not daring to step too far upon a floor I cannot be sure about, I squat to take photos through the apertures offered, and realise the extent of the castle, its maze of rooms, lobbies, stories, missing roofs! I retrace my steps towards the spiral stair-case, and in amazement discover that the very steps to which I have just trusted my weight and life, my ponderous life so to say, are only resting on some rare granite gravels by chance still in place, the rest of the liberty-prone masonry having disap-peared, leaving ample room for light com-ing from the opposite loophole to flow through. Wisely I change my mind, and decide not to go further upstairs this how-ever enticing tower. Consequently I trust again my ponderous life to the said steps to spiral downstairs. Now I push my way fur-ther inside the castle, walk along a some-how narrow very long corridor, which must have been the spine of the castle, crossing intersecting numerous interconnecting cor-ridors. The tumbled down masonry is op-pressive, the narrow dim passage is not re-assuring, the noises of my progress creep up my limbs, fill my head with worrying thoughts, am I alone? Am I really alone in this maze of walls and corridors? Fresh clues of strewn beer cans and old cigarette packs fuel my doubts, and the empty and dark embrasures I pass in front of, quicker now, become more and more menacing! Uneasiness is tangible to such an extent that I stop to eavesdrop... nothing. Nothing, but since the tricky spiral staircase episode, snatches of gothic literature keep coming to my mind! The wall of my imagination, from liquid becomes dense, then truly solid! It slows me down, then stops me, suddenly becoming dark and thick. Time to go back, and without yielding to panic retrace one's steps! Once outside and having correctly squeezed through the wire netting breach, I can now turn round and objectively, Cartesian-ly, reassuringly reconsider the ruins of Slains castle! After all, these are only building ruins, but however, after those few minutes spent in their midst, they assume a mysterious and worrying hue. Alright, few more photos, then back to our camper by the carriage drive. My first words to Françoise are: "Impressive this castle!"

Of course Boswell and Johnson's experience in 1773 must have been very different. The castle was in a good shape, so the people inhabiting it. I decide to buy a Loto ticket in order to have one chance over forty nine millions to give it back its former glory[2]. Here they were received, met and spoke to Mister Boyd, Lord Errol's brother. Mister Boyd had fought at Culloden, not very far, near Inverness. He had managed to flee when the English had crushed them, and go into hiding a whole year on Aran island, far enough from here, near Glasgow, then he had taken refuge twenty years in France, and was living now in Aberdeen with his French wife. They also met Lord Errol, dined with him, he took them to their respective bedrooms, Boswell's one was overlooking the sea, and Boswell remembered Lord Kilmarnock, Lord Errol's father, whose head had been

---

[2] In the 2012 French edition I had written: « A ce jour je ne l'ai pas encore fait, mais je le ferai… on ne sait jamais. ». Now I have done it, but lost!

severed in London in 1746, just after the demise of Culloden!

Peterhead, Fraserburgh, Banff, Cullen, Elgin, Findhorn

And then we went along the coast through Peterhead, picnicked in Fraserburgh. As for them, they had gone through Old Deer, and at Strichen they visited what was called then a Druid's temple, not a menhir but a dolmen according to Boswell's description, unless it was the remnant of a cromlech, there too we will have to come back. They ate with Lord Fraser of Strichen, who asked a servant to put them back by a shortcut on the main road, and they slept at Banff. We drove through Banff and drank tea at Cullen, on the square, where they had taken the morrow their breakfast, dried haddocks broiled, that Johnson had not liked! Indeed Johnson was bulging with prejudices, and as Boswell puts it politely, he tried to *"educate his palate"*, but all in vain. Then as they did we went to Elgin to visit the cathedral, which is as much "ruin-embellished" than the others. But as it was already late, we visited it from the outside of the shut fence only, a grazing setting sun wonderfully enhancing it, and the multitude of tombstones huddling cuddly against it, projecting on the green grass as many dense shadow slabs, taletellers of bygone past and fleeing present. Johnson explains that the lead from the roof had been removed in order to convert it into proper money for the Scottish army, that he thought some private interests had mixed in it, but that when being sailed to Holland where it had to be sold, providence in which he believed had claimed its share, in fact the totality, and had sunk it down! Quite a heavy conclusion!

Boswell and Johnson had slept at Forres where they had found "*an admirable inn*" according to Boswell. As for us, once up to Forres we turned towards the sea, where we found a royal resting place at Findhorn.

Forres, Cawdor, Nairn, Fort George, Inverness, Beauly

On the morrow we drove through Forres, then to Cawdor, Cawdor's castle, Macbeth's castle!

You remember that Macbeth is this guy who with a friend of him is horse riding across a moor on their way back from a battle fought for their king, when they meet three prophesising witches, giving him the title of Thane of Cawdor, and then the one of King of Scotland! And then plop they disappear. And indeed he becomes at once Thane of Cawdor in lieu and place of the one who was so, because this latter is in disgrace, blab, blab, blab, and of course with the second part of the prophesy which makes him King he gets worked up, and with his wife at his side for the best and the worst, they scheme an assassination of the present King, and actually assassinate him, making believe someone else's culpability, but his wife turns mad, and the King's ghost keeps plaguing him, apparitions, remorse, etc., and then the witches come back to tell him that when a certain wood walks he will die, struck by a man not born of woman, quite an enigma, and the walking wood is foolishly a camouflaged army, and the man not born of woman is a bloke born by caesarean, elementary my dear Watson... and voilà you have Macbeth decoded! As for me I would advise you to go and watch it on TV, cinema, or at Stratford upon Avon, it is Shakespeare's and not bad. Now it is said that not everything is true, that he altered some parts and wrote in novel form, which is normal, logical and fair.

Boswell and Johnson knew all this quite well, but they were not impressed. They had slept at Forres, breakfasted at Nairn, then had visited a said Mac Aulay, parson, who had published a book about St. Kilda, the most westerly of Scotland's islands, but they did not think he was the author, just the collector of facts, and after dinner they walked to *"the old castle of Calder"*. Johnson said the highlands to begin at Nairn, because there, for the first time, he saw peat fires and heard the Erse language. This parson suggested also a route for the rest of their trip, with Boswell they spread a map on the table and he pointed out a route for them that Boswell noted down.

But first they went to Fort George, not far, sea side. They had a letter of introduction, were well received, and visited the fort which in fact was brand new, built after the famous battle of Culloden not far, about ten miles away, where you remember Charles Edward Stuart and his highlanders' army were crushed in 1746. About twenty years had been necessary to build it, its main purpose being to prevent any future Jacobite uprising, named such because in fact it supported the descendants of James II of England and Ireland, also called James VII of Scotland because they had already had six James in Scotland, exiled in 1688 when ousted by William of Orange, protestant against this catholic James. So, 1773 minus 1746 makes 27 years— Culloden—27 minus 20 years of construction makes 7 years only! It was really brand new, they were indeed very proud of it! But this pride, probably only English side, is not visible through Johnson's and Boswell's journals. Johnson, who distrusts imagination, other's as well as his own, says that not being a specialist he cannot make a scientific description, and Boswell as usual prefers to tell us about people met, their conversations, and of the "*uncommonly mild and sweet tone of voice*" of the governor's wife. He however fancies himself a "*military man*", romantic Boswell, haloed in glory and state. There they dined, we picnicked. To imagine them there was very easy indeed, because Fort George has never been used against Jacobites, dwindling species, nor against who else by the way, but had rather been a training camp for subsequent imperial armies, and consequently has remained as such, unspoiled, untouched, in its eighteen century's hue, even improved by a methodical mechanical twenty first century's regular mowing of the grass, which spreads over vast expanses where the English hoped to sweep kill mow down by heavy gunfire the furious Jacobites. From there they went to Inverness not far away, we did the same.

At Inverness, at the mouth of the river Ness flowing from the Loch Ness, they "*put up at Mackenzie's inn*". As for us at Inverness, we involuntarily followed the Mackenzie's trail. It was not exactly at Inverness, but at Beauly very close, at the far end of the firth of Beauly. We had two aims. One was to visit someone at Beauly, the second one was to stray away from Boswell and Johnson's trail for a while, and go up north where they had not been. This someone to visit at Beauly were Mary Bell's relatives, MacLennan people like herself. Mrs. Bell and her husband were our neighbours when we used to spend our summer holiday in London with our then very young children Rachel and Luc, swapping houses with the Dolamore family, who with their children slightly older than ours, preferred to go and scorch in the south of France, while we were happy with the London climate. We had then got along very well with our next-door neighbours Bell, she housekeeper, and he former Scotland-Yard superintendent, now at the foreign office, well educated, distinguished and very English, who one evening with his car, had taken us for a by-night tour of London, and the not yet rehabilitated docks area, where we could still smell spices having poured in from the empire's seven seas. He is now old and very sick, and I wanted my wife to see him before he goes to nothingness or the unknown. In this neighbourhood several are already gone, amongst them Sheila, Geoff's wife, our friends Dolamore with whom we used to swap houses. We, human species, have been and are in so deep a way able to alter our natural environment, of creating through techniques an artificial world, of filtering the real world through our culture, that we tend to forget our mortal condition! So, driving up to Scotland we stopped to visit our friends Alan and Mary Bell, and when we told them where we were heading to, Mary gave us the address of her family in Beauly. By chance we park right inside their street! Houses do not have numbers but names, theirs is "Roneval", I find it easily and we tell them who we are. Ann and John willingly invite us to come in and converse. They recall the past, are happy to have some fresh news, to watch photos of their relatives on our digital camera display, and when I disclose that my wife is a Mackenzie, a cousin-like glow illuminates their features, they fetch and show us the MacLennan's panoply, kilt, sporran, belt, shirt, socks and ribbons, ornamented dagger and brooch. A surprise is to discover at the very bottom of the sporran few coins which had been sleeping there for years, we joke about them. And then they tell us that the Mackenzie's chief is very close by, at Strathpeffer indeed! It is on our north route, we cannot not stop there. So on the morrow, after a good night spent along the village's stadium's hedge, to Strathpeffer, Leod castle, seat of the Mackenzie's head!

Strathpeffer, Helmsdale, Forsinard, Thurso

MacKenzie, in Gaelic Mac Coin-
neach, son of handsome man. Chief we are
coming! We find the castle's entrance, a
high wall, an open gate, a lodge on the left,
a trees-lined drive, a sign with the visiting
opening hours, afternoon's. Now it is
morning! I drive on, after all we are not
mere tourists coming to visit just another
castle, no, we are genuine Mackenzie, at
least my wife is, and we are coming to visit
our chief! It is exactly what we say to the
woman driving down the lane, perhaps the
chief's spouse, who consequently gives us
permission to drive up to the castle. This is
what we do, stop at a small grass car park,
incredible lush grass, then on foot up the
gentle slope towards a beautiful castle well
set off in the middle of an enchanting landscape. It is not a stronghold designed to
withstand bellicose troops, but rather a

mansion expressing high social status. Stepping up to the castle we meet a man who when spoken to repeats the opening hours, as we state Françoise's identity he states his, which is nothing else than the clan's chief! He excuses himself to be busy repairing the roof of a garden house, consequently unable to receive us, advises us to approach the Parisian branch of the clannish organisation. I ask the permission to take a photo of him with my Mackenzie-Françoise next to him, granted, two photos, then we are politely showed off and suggested to come back this afternoon during the opening hours! We leave with a feeling of not having been very well received. I think this clan's chief too distinguished and lacking moral brutality befitting men's leaders. Will he be up to the next Highlands' uprising?

Then we continue and drive along the north side of the firth of Cromarty, where we can see petrol pumping installations, spearhead, gem ornamented dagger, which if it were not for pretexted security reasons glued to its scabbard like Mr MacLennan's one, but instead boldly pulled out, with its white threatening ostensibly glowing naked blade, could once more give Scotland its independence!

We continue up to Helmsdale. There we picnicked in the little harbour. From another car a young couple gets out to picnic at the back of their car, my wife comments: "Oh, he touched her bottom! This is very French indeed!" And when they leave we notice that their registration plate is actually French! Very well observed from my Mackenzie-spouse!

It is also at Helmsdale that we decide to stop driving along the coast, and instead push inland through moors, marshes, peat-bogs, via the 897, typical Scots road with passing places. On such roads, the common mistake of foreigners driving on the right side—because Napoleon 1st influenced their country to switch the driving sides—when the passing place is on the right side of the road, is to actually go inside the passing place instead of just stopping up to its height. Not anymore my mistake. Of course the progression on such roads, as soon as there is some traffic, is much slower than on two lanes roads. Sometimes it seems to you that you are constantly stopped, that your progression is flea-hops style, considerably straining your patience! But such narrow roads have also a real charm, closer to nature, to relief, to geography, with happy surprises round the bends, not smoothed like main roads with their verges, no, rather rough and raw, colourful, still with character. Thus through a magnificent landscape of "wild" moors, we progress along the Helmsdale river, driving through tiny hamlets, playing cat and mouse with the railway line up to Forsinard, where it forsakes us to head eastwards when we continue northwards. Thirty eight miles of passing places road, according to my map, which looked far more, but the souvenir looks more too, hurrah the passing places road! And then the normal road again until Thurso, where we treat ourselves with a campsite overlooking the sea.

Dunnet Head, John o'Groats, Duncansby Head, Wick, Dornoch

On the morrow we begin with ex-treme-geographical maps-reader's tourism. Indeed our Mercator projection map tells us that Dunnet Head is the northernmost part of main Scotland, and so we are naturally attracted by such a "performance"! True that once there, along with a bunch of tour-ists here for the same reason, reality match-es the cartographical figment of our imagi-nation, the sea, only the sea capping UK, with the Orkney Islands in sight. And as always seabirds, symbol of freedom and faraway shores, gliding experts, which in no time at all, from the cliffs' bottom soar up above like if thrown into heaven, happi-ly borne in an invisible Aeolian medium, pass us with a mysterious flutter, question-ing gaze and slight twist of their head to appraise us all the better, and mock us sure-ly. I saw some of them swipe down an invisible slide, swiftly disappear behind a rock spur, then suddenly reappear like by magic, evidently deriving pleasure form it!

At Dunnet Head there is also a lighthouse, built by workers working for, or at least following plans drawn by Robert Louis Stevenson's grandfather. The grandfather lighted the mariners' path, and still lights it, the grandson lighted the readers' path, and still lights it. And in the meanwhile, the grandfather's son, Robert Louis' father, was also a lighthouse builder. The calling of this family was really to shine!

Then direction Duncansby Head, this time the easternmost head, we picnic near the castle of Mey, with a beautiful view over the sea.

First we reach John o' Groats, small harbour very close to Duncansby Head. Strange name, and strange name's origin. I would say that in the interactive chain, Technical-Behavioural-Social-Cultural, four angles of a square, the starting point has been the technical possibility to create a ferryboat line between this place and the Orkney Islands, which induced a behavioural change in the local population, increased exchanges with the Orkney, commerce, economy, which in turn induced a social change, emigration-immigration and probably new settlements, with possibly a demographic surge, and a cultural implication with the name of the place which became John o' Groats, because the name of the originator of these interactive changes had been Jan de Groote, which became John of Groats, then "*of*" became o'. He was Dutch, and late XVth century had obtained a royal permission to build a ferryboat line!

From John o' Groats, a short hilly narrow road takes us to Duncansby Head, the most northern-eastern cape of main Scotland. Here also there is a lighthouse, built too I believe by a Stevenson, but whom? Let us to admit though that "*Stevenson*" is somehow the Scots equivalent for French "*Dupont*"! Here we can see seals, plenty of seals, the sea is teeming with seals. I am perhaps exaggerating, but let's say that it is easy to observe them, that they frolic and feel at ease, are really in their milieu, at home. There is sheep too, we share the cape with sheep. And the stony craggy rugged red sandstone cliffs are an ideal habitat for a host of seabirds nesting there, inhabiting, diving, fishing, shouting, flying, re-flying, spinning, majestically gliding, pleasuring, and making you feel, you human being, with all your technical paraphernalia, roads and vehicles, cameras and telephones, binoculars, etc., a mere dwarf. Along these heights hemmed by a roaring white foam, they are giants to whom the same earth, same air, same gentle light, same empty ether they fill with their raucous and doleful cries, belong to.

To the trained eyes, our winged interlocutors have been fulmars, guillemots, puffins, kittiwakes, great-skuas, curlews, wheatears, lapwings, larks, and some unknown.

Voilà that was our diversion, time to
head back to Inverness and resume the
thread of our literary tour, along the coast
this time, through Wick. We reach Wick
late afternoon, and find a genuine "fish and
chips" shop, with a long queue on the
pavement, which progresses fast though,
and indoors a priority queue and bank for
those who have phone-ordered, and a big-
ger bank for those who wish to order now.
It is quite a sight, the cooking and selling
staff is indeed a very young girls team. The
accent it very Scots, there is no time spent
in useless civilities, people know what they
want and in few words the order is made,
really wonderfully well deep-fried copious
fresh bits of fish, along with as well wonderfully fried king-size chips, in successive
waves reach the bank, overflow it, and are
exchanged for few coins by the crowd's
front liners. Amongst the throng are some
children, obviously mission bearers from
home, sometimes anxious to deliver proper-
ly in words the order they are entrusted
with, which order they tirelessly repeat
mentally since they left mum, sometimes

showing at arm's length a scrap of paper depository of the order's secret, that the young frowning girl reads and embarrassingly asks for precisions about. It is our turn, we had time to choose, and make a zero fault by ordering what is best, which is duly handed over to us over the bank at a breaking wave time, that like a long coveted treasure we escort to our camper van, that we park on a small square surrounded by low and simple houses, and while eating we rapture over the excellent taste of the fish, the perfect oil saturation of the chips, and the crusty texture of the coating. We match our royal meal with a perfectly flavoured cider, and exclaim "isn't it nice here?!" To have simple tastes might lead to great pleasures!

Auto gratified so, we continue our way towards Inverness, driving through Helmsdale where we had left the coast to plunge through marshes, peat, moor, via the narrow road with passing places. Then along Loch Fleet by a small by road, reaching Dornoch where between a golf course and a campsite we camped near the sea. On the morrow morning, rested, we discover that once more, but this time without malice aforethought because we had not seen the sign, we slept on a "no overnight parking"! When leaving, attracted by a small sign "aerodrome", we follow the road to it at the mouth of the firth of Dornoch. It is Saturday the 30th of July, and in preparation is an aeronautical fair. I discuss awhile with the organisers-participants-pilots who are expecting people today, introducing myself as the due homebuilder-owner-pilot of a Flying Flea, a legendary plane well-known of course also under Scots' latitudes, am invited to participate to their fair, but as on the one hand my spouse is not what we could qualify an aeronautical fan, and on the other hand we are keen to pick up again Boswell and Johnson's trail, we decline their offer and continue our way, reaching in the morning Inverness not far away now.

Inverness, Falls of Fiers,
Fort Augustus, Glen of Moriston,
Ratagan, Glenelg

Inverness for the second time, in fact for the third. Because it was... oh, something like fifteen years ago, that with our daughter Noémie we had been "up" to Inverness already. We had only a tent at that time, and the weather was not very nice nor very hot. We had visited the site of Culloden, where the Highlanders army, exhausted by a useless nocturnal walk, starving by lack of supply-services, and because of a slightly excited Charles who instead of following his wise generals telling him that they had time to prepare for the battle, had hustled his army, had sermonised it to be on the field, a very bad field, as early as possible, when its exhaustion state was passed sermonising, and that facing them there was a Cumberland knowing the sorry state of Charles' army which had attempted by a long trying and useless because not fast enough nocturnal walk, to attack his camp at Nairn... it was a catastrophe! Nowadays on the battlefield there are little signs telling where such and such clans were, and I wanted to know—then perfectly ignorant of the important role the Mackenzie's had played in this uprising—whether they were Charles or the English's side. Now my past ignorance makes me blush, but then with my wife Françoise Mackenzie we had played a game, running from sign to sign to know whether we were going to divorce, having declared that in the eventuality of a Mackenzie's betrayal, I could not possibly abide by my marital vows! But the sign was perfectly clear, the Mackenzie clan had indeed partaken of their sufferings, their torn bodies, their ripping anguishes, their disappointed wishes, and their casualties of course, and then their shameful retreat, Bonnie Prince Charlie's fate. And those who escaped with their lives remained to undergo the terrible after-Culloden persecutions, when the victorious English forbade them to wear clans colours, tartans, weap-

ons, songs and bagpipes, their whole clannish culture, forfeited their territories,
stripped Highlanders of whatever was their
soul.

Boswell and Johnson were at Inverness only 27 years after the battle. They
did not visit the field of Culloden, no car
park, no reception desk, no tickets to be
bought, no tourist shops, no signs and foot-
paths, only unspoiled moor like the very
day of the battle!

From Inverness they went to Fort
Augustus, the other end of Loch Ness. By
which road? Johnson in his journal mentions waterfalls, "Fiers's", that I could not
find on our map. I could find others, well
plotted west side of the Loch where a
"normal" road goes. Strange, all the more
strange as he describes them as *the cele-
brated fall of Fiers*. On the other bank of
the Loch, east-side, there is only a "passing-
places" road, yes indeed, but there is also
about mid-lake on our map a place called
"Foyers". On this slim clue I ground my

choice for this narrow road, never mind the delay, guessing also that the normal road going through Glen More must be more recent than the one going through The Great Glen. The weather is nice, who says it is always raining in Scotland ?... and just before Dores, with a wonderful view over the well-known Nessie's loch, a post Boswell and Johnson's invention, we stop to picnic. And then, from passing place to passing place, we progress until Foyers where, oh miracle, there are indeed waterfalls not mentioned on my three miles to one inch map. So there it is, only because they are not connected up by a normal road allowing a normal flow of normal tourists, they are unnamed on a normal roadmap. Aren't we slightly manipulated? But who presides over these manipulations? Assuredly sincere people aiming at the welfare of the most numerous! Everything is a matter of roads...

In Boswell and Johnson's times they were well connected up, as far as roads were concerned, and consequently were a prime touristic destination for an elite only. One of the small explanatory boards tells: "The Falls were one of Scotland's top three sights for lovers of wild landscapes. From the 1730s, Wade's military road along Loch Ness made Foyers easier to visit." And also that "Dr Johnson and James Boswell visited the Falls of Fiers' in 1773" There is a short excerpt from Johnson's journal, and an enumeration of literary well-known figures having visited and praised the falls. Indeed Boswell and Johnson had travelled this side of the loch, which today is the discreet one! We admire the falls, and then as they did, continue towards Fort Augustus where they were received by the governor, and where we saw a thriving tourism, well connected up by roads, and a canal which did not exist then, and a now missing Fort.

At Inverness they had given up their comfortable chaise to hire horses and guides instead. They were four horses and five human beings. Joseph Ritter, James' domestic, a well-travelled hefty bohemian speaking several languages, James Boswell himself, lowland Scotsman, known by name in these remote corners thanks to his father's rounds as a judge in the Highlands, Samuel Johnson, lexicographer, reviewer, literary man, moralist, conversationalist, eighteen century's media star, a potent embodiment of his time's ideas and prejudices, Englishman, three of them on horseback, a fourth horse carrying luggage, because at that time to be clean was not to take a shower, but change underwear, two Highlanders walking at their sides, Lauchlan Vass and John Hay, and regarding horses I do not have their names. On the morrow at Fort Augustus they declined the governor's invitation to dine, instead they set off at around noon to go not too far off at Anoch, where there was an inn, the last one before their trip westward towards the sea. The governor's name I suppress, because he is an army man, and on the top of that of French extraction, and sold to the English! Here they dined, supped, slept, and chatted with the landlord who, also a tenant-farmer, was toying with the idea of emigrating, because rents had become really too high after the Culloden disaster.

On the morrow they had a long road ahead of them through Glen Moriston, then Loch Cluanie, then the slope down towards Loch Duich which is in fact the way to the sea, and then the climb of Ratagan Mountain where Johnson had the fright of his life, when his tired horse faltered and he contemplated himself at the precipice's bottom. He laconically reports in his journal: "*and I called in haste to the Highlander to hold him.*" Late afternoon, before ascending Ratakan, they had stopped at a village, Auchnasheal according to Boswell, Auknasheals according to Johnson, Ault-a-chrinn according to Maradène, where they ate two dishes of milk, and dealt out wheat bread and tobacco to the inhabitants gathered around them, bread and tobacco governor Trapaud of Fort Augustus, the very same whom I suppressed the name not long ago, but well, even amongst army men there are some nice people, which is indeed one of the numerous unyielding contradic-

tions of our world, had told them to carry
with them, and where Johnson got some
change out of his shilling from Joseph and
the accompanying guides interpreters Highlanders, then had all children lined up in
order to allot a coin each, which must have
been quite a sight! It is also earlier this day
that Johnson, at a resting stop for horses in
need of a good grazing, "*conceived the
thought of this narration*", his journal, in
these remote wild regions with forbidding
summits.

The climb of Ratagan is indeed
quite impressive, I advise heavy recreational vehicle's owners against it. Some bends
have been cut, contemptuously leaving
aside stretches of the narrow old road which
is spanning rivulets by charming little stone
bridges, still crowned with parapet rem-
nants. I am so sure that they went this way
up with their grumbling Johnson that we
park our van, and I amble few meters on
this very same road, aware of following
their "horse steps". Before the pass we stop
once more, this time to feast our eyes on

loch Duich. Then it is the comparatively gentle slope down to Glenelg, where we bivouac in front of the soldiers' memorial, lulled by the splashes of the sea still intervening between us and the Isle of Skye.

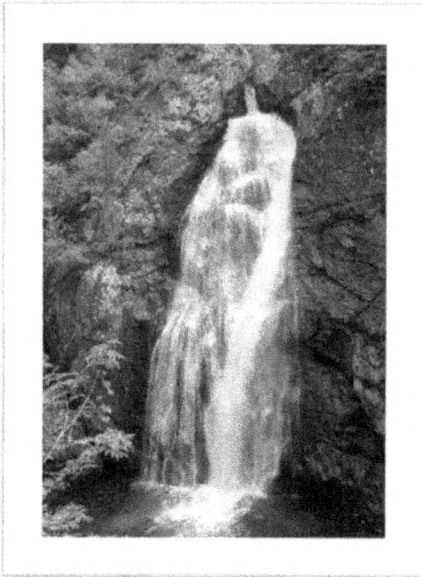

Falls of Fiers

Ferry-boat Glenelg-Skye

Our 1773's travellers had taken a ferry-boat from Glenelg to Armadale, which is south of the Isle of Skye. In 2011 such a link does not exist. But was it really a ferry-boat with a regular plying? Of course not, all they say is "*Having procured a boat*" according to Johnson, and "*we got into a boat*" for Boswell. Indeed it was far from a constant flow of tourists being plied one way or the other. On reaching Glenelg, Boswell mentions that they passed near the barracks of Bernéra, as for us on the morrow, it is precisely this direction we take when following signs to go to the ferry-boat terminal. The road again is really very narrow, and a sign says that the barracks cannot be visited because in a sorry state of tumbling down. Anyhow, we don't even descry these barracks! And we reach the end of the road turning right into water!

A last bend on the left, a gentle slope down towards a booth also on the left, straight ahead a small lighthouse, on the right a concrete slipway courageously reaching into the transparent water, and in some distance a metallic floating machine which seems to be the ferry-boat. Next to the courageous slipway there is a moored boat. A man comes, jolly, whistling, full of life and buoyancy, from his car he lets out two dogs, ferry-boat dogs, open the booth, open the small lighthouse, the circular ground floor room of which is a tourists shop of the sort "help yourself and put your money inside the honesty-box, as for me I have no time to attend to you, I have other fish to fry if you wish to cross", and under the concerned gaze of his two dogs with whom I am playing, he uses the boat to go to the floating machine some way off that seems to be the ferry-boat, starts its engine which on waking up is very recalcitrant, and shows its bad mood at being woken up so, by prolixly and joyfully belching out an abundant and opaque smoke up its funnel. I am playing with the two dogs of which the

youngest, less worried, likes my throwing
of gravels or small pieces of wood he eagerly catches and sulkily brings back, willing
to give them back but feigning not to, so
that in turn I feign to pilfer them, then
throw them again. Another car is coming,
then another one I think, all customers for
the first crossing. We had arrived somehow
early, ignorant of the crossings' schedule,
of everything in fact about this charming
and tiny and non-commercial ferryboat,
which boasts to date back to Boswell and
Johnson's passage, and while waiting for
the opening of the line, have breakfasted in
the comfort of our camper. While the engine of the ferry is warming up and that, to
the great joy of the dogs, the ferry is steered
to the quay, or rather the slope, we shop, in
the help yourself and honesty payment
style, a mug, "Over the sea to Skye,
Glenelg-Skye, Ferry", and some postcards.
I also write a short entry on their logbook.
The platform of the metallic floating machine rotates around an axis so that to land
on the concrete slope, inviting cars to come
aboard! Another man has joined the crew,

the two dogs also, and our small camper proudly goes aboard. The crossing lasts only few minutes against a lateral current obviously violent, which is not a problem for the engine now fully woken up, with its clear song and its relatively transparent smoke, long enough however to communicate with the crewmember who is curious to know whether every night we stop at campsites or camp in the wild. I take this opportunity to ask him about the Bernéra barracks, of which Boswell says *"there was only a serjeant and few men there"*, and he finger points them to me! We very nearly "missed" them, but once on the other shore, Skye Island's shore, through binoculars we observe and photograph them. They were built after the 1715's Jacobite uprising, in order to prevent any new insurrectional army supposed to have swollen on Skye, to cross at this narrow place. Now we are on Skye, not where they landed, but on Skye however.

Flora Macdonald

Skye, a mere island amongst Scots islands, but also a Scotland of its own, not really anymore today, but in the past certainly. It was a trustworthy reservoir of fearless, sentimental, naïve men, during the said insurrectional wars, when the English octopus was stifling the struggling Scots eel. As well as Raasay Island, it also was a refuge for Bonnie Prince Charlie, when women and men took mighty risks, braved the English and despised huge rewards for his capture, to instead allow him to escape and reach douce France. I do not know as for you, but I find it hard to understand the feelings of loyalty towards a power eager aristocrat, leading simple Highlanders to die quartered, decapitated, or worm-eaten aboard prison boats kindly provided for them by the victorious English. There is so much irrational in the behaviour of the sometimes rational human animal! The philosophers' approach in their attempt at understanding him, lies in fact in a mere description of the apparent reasons of his unreason. But we reach the bottom of the pot when we do not understand the reasons of those who accepted to be boiled in it. And historians try only to objectively decipher the ingredients of the historic soup. There, our two associate heroes, Boswell and Johnson, are readers-actors-writers. Readers of a recent history, actors through the feelings moving them, and writers of their journals which are primary sources to historians and philosophers. It is a mere twenty seven years after the events, both of them say to feel nostalgia for the bygone order, and both of them have written an account of their tour. And there in Skye Island, they met a witness-actor of fleeing Bonnie! They slept where Bonnie had slept, and Johnson even in his very same bed! They were at Kingsburgh, at Miss Flora Macdonald's place, now wife of Mr Macdonald, or "Kingsburgh", because traditionally named after his land. She told them how they had disguised Bonnie in a servant girl, with dress and all, how he used to lift his dress too high when fording rivulets, that he was supposed to be an Irish girl named Betty Bourke, hired by no one else than herself, Flora Macdonald, and that in such a disguise and association they travelled unnoticed under the English's very nose. Sometimes history is funny.

And as for us when we reach Kingsburgh, I thought we would find something about Flora, monument, plaque, commemoration, house... Kingsburgh is a very small place, a cul-de-sac of few houses, farms. But nothing, at first sight nothing! Wind blowing and unfair weather. We have summarily parked in front of a bunch of houses, I take another look at my primary literary sources of Boswell and Johnson's journals, dive into them to ascertain that it is this Kingsburgh they are speaking about, yes it is, feel perplexed, and then a car tries to get out of a farm we partly blockade, before the driver could manoeuvre clear I am out with my question: "would you know where Flora Macdonald's house is?". Inside the car a young couple, Mister is driving, Mistress at the back with baby. The man lowers his window, shows me direction to go on foot some distance, in fact he does not know exactly where, then tells that his parents know and used to go there, by chance his parents just arrive, tell us how to go closer by car, then climb over a fence, cross a property with sheep, slope down a little towards a long stone wall sliding to the sea, a gap, a gate, there, right behind and among ferns, probably nothing more visible than a heap of stones, Flora's house! I find everything exactly as they told me, I am delighted, and indeed nothing really is visible, no monument plaque or commemoration, nor a house, but a site, a magical historical site I soak myself in, feast on. I look at the sea-arm with Flora's eyes, listen to the wind with Johnson's ears, and breathe in with Boswell's lungs. I linger there, take photos, and unwillingly slowly retrace my steps towards our vehicle. Why is there nothing there, not even a plaque? Stuarts, if there are still some of them, are perhaps under surveillance! Is

there some intelligence with opposed interests scared of pilgrimage sites, may-be?
What a piece of luck to have been guided to
this very spot...!

What between Raasay and Skye,
Boswell and Johnson stayed about one
month, well received by chieftains having
lost their authority, jurisdiction, aura, and
paying high rents for the lease of their lands
to a greedy aristocracy. In consequence, at
a time when America looked like an Eldo-
rado, their tenants were emigrating with
their families and belongings to try their
luck on the other side of the Atlantic. One
year after their visit, Flora, with her seven
children and her husband, did the same, but
with a mitigated success which made them
cross back home, settle again in Skye and
live there for the rest of their lives. As for
us we stayed only two days, after Kingsburgh we went up to the top of the Isle of
Skye, paid a visit to Flora's resting place, a
funeral monument apparently paid by an
1880's subscription, had a glimpse at the
low thatched houses which were the high-

landers' abode of the time, stopped to pick up two hitchhikers wearing kilts, one of which was a Mackenzie's, but they were ignorant of it as they were in fact two young Frenchmen disguised in Scotsmen, and then had bivouac at the campsite of Portree, le Port du Roi, King's harbour, because James V had landed there.

...a visit to Flora's resting place,

Ullinish, Dunvegan, Talisker, Armadale

On the morrow, the first of August, we went to Ullinish, where they had sur- veyed a Broch. Nowadays we know more about Broches than in their times, they were big circular habitats of several storeys with a wooden structure, with stone double walls like thermos bottles, dating back from around 2300 to 1900 years! We continued until Dunvegan, where they had been enter- tained at the castle which nowadays is also visited by busloads of Chinese people, which visit is by the way interesting, Mac- Leod's seat. On our way down we stopped at Talisker, which revolves around its whis- ky, already brewed here when they visited it in 1773!

All along our literary tour we no- ticed laconic small signs mentioning the visit of Samuel Johnson and James Boswell

here and there in 1773, laconic but respect-
ful. Except here in Talisker, where for the
first and only time, I had a real pleasure of
reading a critical and un-ingratiating commentary on the terrible person Johnson was,
hypochondriac, unenthusiastic, condescend-
ing educated Englishman visiting a savage
country, poor and backward, and I hail the
woman or man who had probably read
Johnson's journal, to dare abandon the ob-
sequious rut followed by the majority impressed by conventional honours, and with
good sense write a courageous critical
commentary. Thank you.

Then, after food shopping in Corry,
French tourists need also to sustain themselves, after having with a French credit
card withdrawn English money from a cash
dispenser, I am sure that a Johnson indeed
very modern in economy would have loved
this, we went down to Armadale, their entry
and exit point to Skye in 1773, where on
the bound to Mallaig car ferry's wharf car
park, we slept. A good surprise was that
the road between Corry and Armadale is

not anymore a narrow road with passing places, as indicated on our 1995's roadmap, but that Europe's money has invested there into a wide wonderfully well surfaced and virtually unused road, which after all these days spent driving on the English and Scots' roads, reminded us of our douce France with its so well paved roads!

Broch of Dun Beag

Mallaig, Fort William, Loch Lomond, Balloch

Well, we have not seen everything, everything they had seen, but we have followed most of their footsteps, and it is not finished. They had sailed to Coll, then Mull, and Ulva and Inch Kenneth, to Iona called then Icolmkill, which had been the stepping stone of the Christian faith in these remote parts. But we are in a hurry, must head back home, and instead land at Mallaig just in front, to take the road leading to Fort William, where out of vexation we visit charity shops. Then southwards by the 82's, to pick up again their trail along Loch Lomond, and in these civilised areas, not far from Glasgow, we sleep at the campsite of Balloch, big and luxurious, where plots have electricity, and where because of human beings supernumerary, confidence yields to defiance, which made me leave a deposit for a length of an electric extension they lent me! And I am realising now, in the comfort of my "writer's" study, when reading again Johnson, that they slept here as well, "*Where the Loch discharges itself into a river, called the Leven,*"! On the morrow it is by post chaise that they went to Glasgow.

Glasgow

In Glasgow they visited the cathedral, of course, which is the only one still standing in Scotland after the civil disorders accompanying the religions dissensions. As everybody knows, words are of momentous importance, and there again it is "words" which saved the cathedral. When a crowd came to destroy the "cathedral", an executive cleric told them: "But look, this is not a cathedral, only several churches stitched together!" "Oh" said the crowd, "in that case let it be!" and there it is! It reminds me that in Beijing an important Buddhist temple avoided destruction because it was barricaded with a big poster of Mao, and that in order to enter and destroy it, it would have been necessary to pull down the said poster first. We also visited the cathedral of Glasgow. Thanks to the help of our Global Positioning System, we first entered the city's heart through a vena cava, were ejected into the arterial system through an aorta, then guided from arteries to arterioles, and managed to park nearby the cathedral. The anecdote is that the weather was fine, that I found a pew forgotten green umbrella, ostentatiously walked it around this huge overloaded cathedral, then took it to our camper, its new home, where between my spouse and myself it has now the evocative name of "Glasgow".

Loudoun

After Glasgow where they had met a fashionable society, they went to Loudoun, to be received by the earl of Loudoun, *"and by the countess his mother, who, in her ninety-fifth year, had all her faculties quite unimpaired."* On our map no Loudoun! But while driving on the 77's, heading towards Kilmarnock, I saw a sign advertising "Loudoun Castle Theme Park"! And what if this Loudoun castle were our Loudoun? The analogy is worthwhile an investigating detour... So we followed the signs leading to an entrance shut by a monumental iron gate, with as only possible clue a phone number for deliveries. The theme park is closed! It is past noon, meal time, so I park our van French way on the wrong side of the entrance, and we picnic inside the comfort of our recreational vehicle. I read again our authors' journals, find the similitude of names really puzzling, and consider the audacity of calling the "for deliveries" number, of stating my identity and quality of "researcher", after all this very same year, as part of my university curriculum, I have benefited by a CNRS subsidy to go to Stratford upon Avon! And while my spouse is dissuading me, a car drives down the alley, a woman steps out to open the gate, I jump out of our van with my e-reader still in hands, greet the woman, tell her I am French, to which she answers "I know"!, briefly expose my quest, and she, slightly irritated, lofty and like in a hurry, replies "You may go up to the castle but no further, alright?, and when you leave do not forget to shut the gate!", which in fact is maintained locked by a chain without padlock passing through both hangings. "Yes yes, thank you very much!" and stirred up I go up to the castle's ruins, without coming too close I take photos, am delighted, and as planned shut the iron gate behind us, leaving a post-it of thanks to the haughty lady of the manor, and once more wonder at our persistent good luck!

Dundonald

And then they stopped, not very far
from there, at Mr Campbell of Treesbank's,
who was married to Boswell's sister in law.
Boswell was here on known grounds, near
Auchinleck, his home. As for Johnson, after their courageous and uncomfortable
long and complicated journey in the Highlands, their perilous navigations and daring
exploration of the Hebrides, he loved the
company and comfort of Lowland aristocrats' houses. The day after the morrow,
Boswell urged a becoming lazy Johnson to
pay a visit to the Countess of Eglintoune,
just few miles away. On their way there,
they climbed up to the ruins of the Castle of
Dundonald which had been *"one of the
many residencies of the kings of Scotland"*.
Inside the nice little museum at its foot, I
take of photo of a pre-restoration model of
the castle, assuming that in 1773, when
visitors were scarce and far apart in time,

the castle must have looked like that. It is assuredly in such a landscape of tumbling walls that Johnson's roars of laughter at the simple accommodation of ancient Scots Kings echoed. This very same evening they were at James Boswell's place in Auchinleck.

Auchinleck

And now, icing on the cake, I really wanted to see "Boswell's house" in Auchinleck. To Auchinleck we wend. Auchinleck is a soulless village, and when we ask for "Boswell's house", we are directed to the pub, Boswell's arms! All we find about Boswell is this pub and one street. Here nobody knows our hero. Instead we are guided towards a mansion recently refurbished and open to the public, Dumfries', not far away, where we go, drive into the park through the open deliveries' entrance, come closer, nobody there, but I do not recognise the picture etched into my brain, I however take photos, and drive out without having been able to inquire from anybody! But no, Dumfries' is not Boswell's house! Back to Auchinleck, incomprehension and surprise at the general ignorance, chance discovery of an along the road exhibition stating that until recently

Auchinleck was an open field coal mine, funny indeed when you know that Johnson explains that Auchinleck means "*stony field*", and that Boswell corrects by saying that it means "*field of flagstone*", but no Boswell's house! Tiredness and discouragement! It is becoming late and thirsty and hot, I would like an ice-cream, and anyhow we need some shopping, so at the traffic light we drive once again passed Boswell's arms and go to the supermarket nearby. Hagendass ice-cream and some shopping, and at the till again I inquire "Boswell's house?" The young woman does not know it, but perhaps her friend does? She queries. No, nothing, perfectly unknown this Boswell! Here in Auchinleck! But maybe this other friend knows? No, bad luck…

Then at the next checkout arrives a couple older than this young generation, and this same young cashier who indeed is concerned by my quest, asks them, and yes, they know! I am incredulous, have they really understood what I am looking for,

"Boswell's house"? Yes, without any doubt, we are talking about the same thing, the same house, the same Boswell! Explanations, and on the map they show me, yes, I know, we already severally passed this sharp bend where he says we must turn into a private path and continue…, but he kindly insists to guide us there, "follow us", alright, small red convertible car that we are following on a car track indeed "private", where we would not have dared to drive by ourselves, then we park beside disused farm buildings, because where John wants to lead us there is a sign "No vehicle allowed", and on foot we continue a dark muddy path, the evening light failing to filter through the dense wood we are crossing, then suddenly a clearing, a nice lawn, and here, here on the left, no doubt, it is the picture I know and recognise, Boswell's house, Boswell's family seat! I am positively delighted! After our long unfruitful search, it is a miracle! Indeed this is it, thank you Michael. I take photos, feast my eyes, he explains that when young he used to play inside the derelict house, that it is now part of Scotland's heritage, that few times per year it opens to visitors. We walk round it, and photos again. And then driving a tractor a young man arrives, gets off, and my guide warns me "he will probably inquire what we are doing here", he does, and in the very polite Anglo-Saxon's way he says "may I help you?", to which I eagerly answer by explaining my quest, my interest in Boswell's family while concluding our literary tour, my wish to write a small university work on the topic, and then he promptly removes his cap and introduces himself with a "I am a Boswell"! Unbelievable, for an icing on the cake, it is an icing! Thank you so much!

ISBN 978-2-9536714-6-9

www.ingramcontent.com/pod-product-compliance
Lightning Source LLC
Chambersburg PA
CBHW070519030426
42337CB00016B/2017